May
18

The 138th day of the year (139th in leap years). There are 227 days remaining until the end of the year.

by Michael Dobson

Timespinner
Press

This book is also available in e-book form for Kindle, e-pub devices, and other formats from your favorite online booksellers.

For more information about the series, about us, or about your special day, please email us at editor@timespinnerpress.com.

Look for other volumes in *The Story of a Special Day*, coming often. See www.timespinnerpress.com for details and for the most recent information.

Table of Contents

Cover: *The Emperor Napoleon in His Study at the Tuileries* by Jacques-Louis David. Napoleon was proclaimed Emperor of France on May 18, 1804 — the COVER STORY and EVENT OF THE DAY.

Quote of the Day

"No man is liberated from fear who dare not see his place in the world as it is; no man can achieve the greatness of which he is capable until he has allowed himself to see his own littleness."

Bertrand Russell, philosopher and mathematician
born May 18, 1872

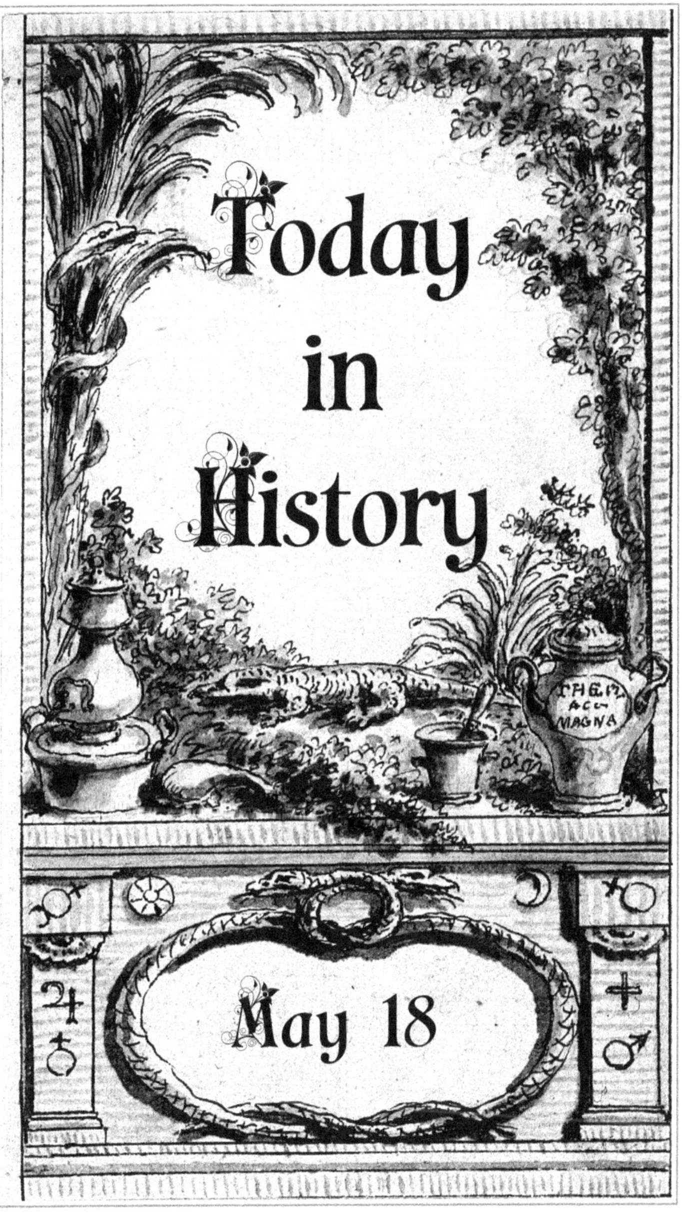
Today
in
History
May 18

Detail from *The Coronation of Napoleon*, by Jacques-Louis David and Georges Rouget (Courtesy Louvre Museum)

What Happened on May 18?

From the creation of great works of engineering and art, to devastating wars and natural disasters, thousands of years of history have left their mark on each and every day of the year. Here are some additional important events that occurred on May 18. (Illustrated items are shaded.)

Cover Story/Event of the Day
Napoleon Becomes Emperor of France

On May 18, 1804, the Senate of the First French Republic voted to make First Consul Napoleon Bonaparte the Emperor of the French.

Born August 15, 1769, he was a young military officer when the French Revolution broke out in 1789. He achieved distinction in the field, and was promoted rapidly during a series of wars that followed the revolution.

By 1794 he was a general, and the following year put down a royalist insurrection. A series of brilliant miltary campaigns gave him increased political influence, and in 1799 he overthrew the revolutionary government, taking the title "First Consul."

After a series of assassination attempts, he decided to create an imperial system based on ancient Rome. By overwhelming vote in a popular referendum, he was elected Emperor.

His coronation took place on December 2, 1804. There were two crowns involved: a laurel wreath, which he wore as he entered the ceremony, and a replica of the crown worn by Charlemagne.

Contrary to legend, he did not crown himself, but lifted the crown above his head, as he was already wearing the wreath. Instead, he placed the crown on the head of his wife Josephine.

His reign would last until 1814, when he was forced to abdicate after his defeat in the War of the Sixth Coalition. He was exiled to the island of Elba, where he escaped the following year. Reclaiming his title, he raised a popular army, but on June 18, 1815, he was defeated at the Battle of Waterloo.

Exiled once again, to the small island of Saint Helena, he remained until his death on May 5, 1821. In 1840, his remains were returned to Paris where they are on display in *Les Invalides*.

The Tomb of Napoleon (Photo: Remy Overkempe, CC BY-SA 3.0)

Other May 18 Events

1152 — The future King **Henry II** of England marries **Eleanor of Aquitaine**.

1291 — With the fall of the city of Acre, the Crusader-controlled Kingdom of Jerusalem ends, **the last attempt by European Christians to control the Holy Land**.

The Siege of Acre, by Dominique Papety

1652 — **Rhode Island** becomes the first colony in English-speaking North America to **outlaw slavery.**

1811 — In a key moment in the campaign for Uruguayan independence, revolutionary forces triump at the **Battle of Las Piedras**. *(Photo page 38.)*

1860 — **Abraham Lincoln** wins the **Republican Party nomination** for President of the United States.

Abraham Lincoln in 1860 (Photo: Alexander Hessler)

1896 — In the case of ***Plessy v. Ferguson***, the US Supreme Court declares that the **"separate but equal"** doctrine is constitutional.

1912 — The **first Indian film**, *Shree Pundalik,* is released in Mumbai.

1926 — Evangelist **Aimee Semple McPherson** disappears in a reported kidnapping, resulting in a national media frenzy. She turns up unharmed five weeks later, and is accused of perpetrating a hoax.

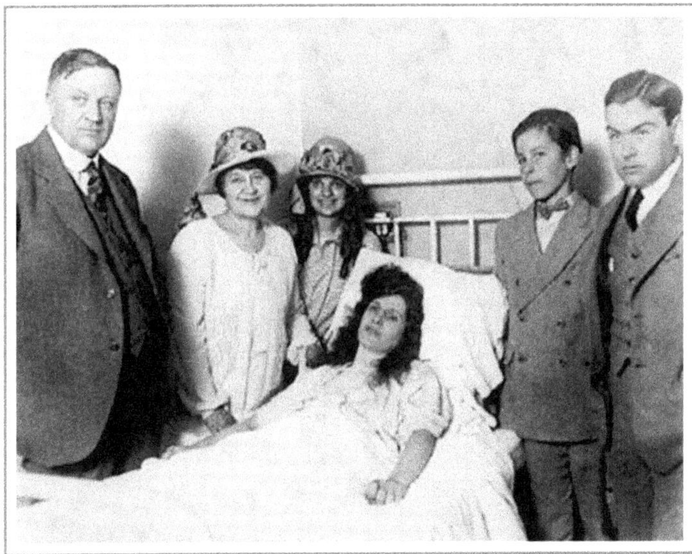

Aimee Semple McPherson in the hospital following her claimed escape from her kidnappers (Credit: International News Photo)

1944 — The World War II **Battle of Monte Cassino** ends with the retreat of German forces. Over 55,000 Allies and 20,000 Germans become casualties in the 123-day long battle.

1953 — Aviator **Jackie Cochran** becomes the **first woman to break the sound barrier.**

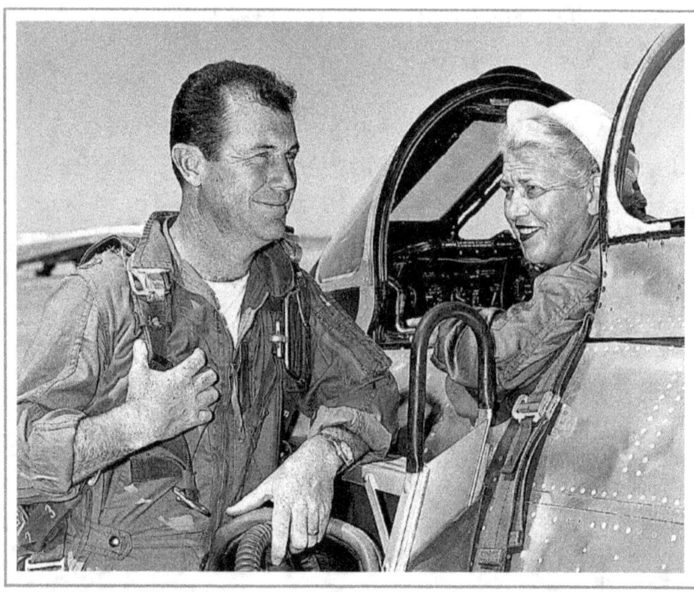

Jackie Cochran (right) with Chuck Yeager in the F-86 jet she flew in becoming the first woman to break the sound barrier

1969 — The **Apollo 10** mission, a "dress rehearsal" for the moon landing that will take place two months later, lifts off.

1974 — **India detonates its first nuclear weapon**, the sixth nation to do so.

2009 — The **Sri Lankan Civil War** ends after nearly 26 years. *(See also page 40 and 41.)*

May, by Hans Thoma

Quote of the Day

"Everybody has to die, but I always believed an exception would be made in my case."

William Saroyan, novelist
died May 18, 1981

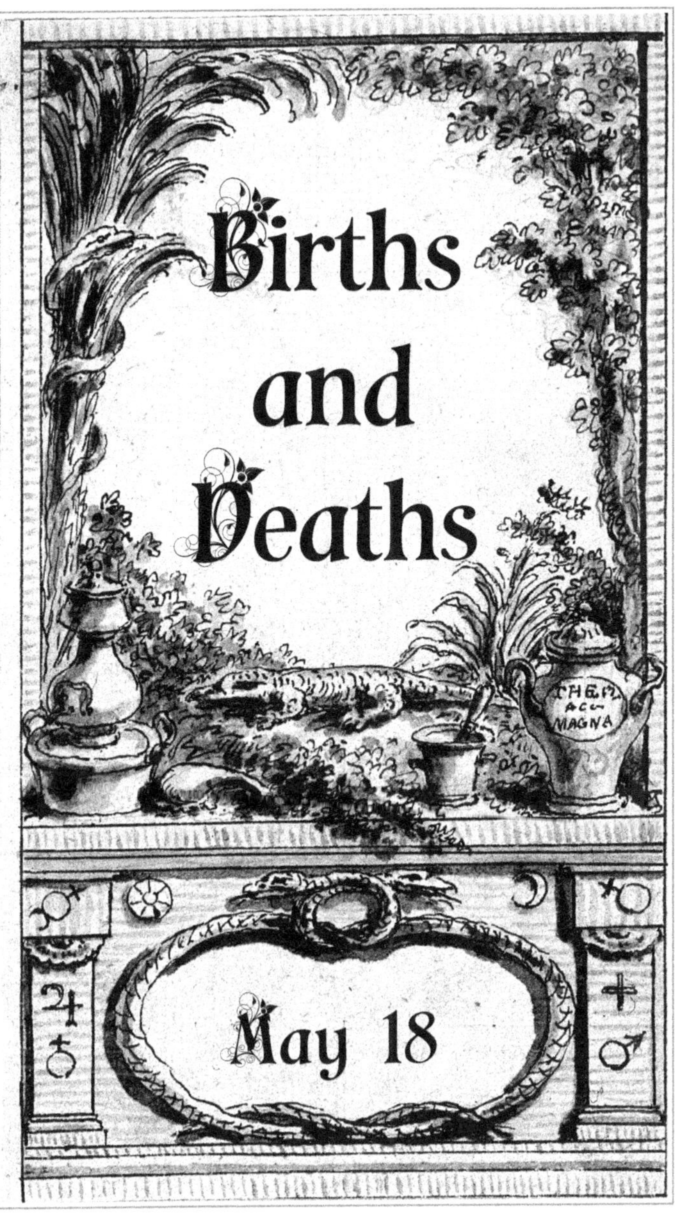# Births and Deaths

May 18

Frank Capra (right, with Captain Roy Boulting), filmmaker who directed *It's a Wonderful Life* and *Mr. Smith Goes to Washington*, in 1944 as a colonel with the US Army Signal Corps editing a war documentary. Capra was born May 18, 1897.

Notable May 18 People

With the current world population at about seven billion people, on average about 19 million people also celebrate their birthdays on May 18 — and that isn't counting the millions and millions who came before! No matter when you were born, you share your birthday with many special people whose accomplishments (and occasionally embarrassments) have been noted as part of history.

In this section, you'll meet fascinating people who share your birthday. They're organized by what they're famous for, and then in reverse chronological order from most recent to earliest. Those who are shown in photographs or artwork have a box around them. We don't have photos of everyone, so please forgive us if your favorite person is missing.

Some of these people you've heard of, others may be new to you, but they all make up an important part of the reason that May 18 is a truly special day!

Pope John Paul II (Photo: Rafic Abou Fadel, CC BY-SA 3.0)

Who Was Born on May 18?

Person of the Day
Pope John Paul II (1920)

Karol Józef Wojtyła, better known as Pope John Paul II, was born in the Polish town of Wadowice on May 18, 1920. The second longest-serving pope in modern history, John Paul II became a highly influential world leader responsible for transforming the modern Roman Catholic Church. He was canonized in 2013, and is sometimes called Saint John Paul the Great by Catholics.

He began studying for the priesthood in a clandestine seminary during the Nazi occupation of Poland during World War II, becoming a priest shortly after the end of the war. He asked his students to call him "Uncle" rather than "Father" because the Communist government forbade priests to travel with students. He became Bishop and later Archbishop of Kraków, and was part of the Second Vatican Council that made historic reforms to Catholicism before being promoted once again to Cardinal in 1967.

As a cardinal, he voted to elect his predecessor, John Paul I, who died after only 33 days in office. In the subsequent conclave, he was made the 264th pope and the first non-Italian pope in 455 years.

As pope he traveled widely, visiting 129 countries. His visit to his homeland of Poland helped spark the Solidarity movement that led to the end of Communist rule. He made major contributions to

Catholic theology, and spoke against apartheid and other crimes against humanity. He made great strides in reconciling the Catholic Church with Judaism and Islam.

In 1981, he was shot and nearly killed by a member of a militant Turkish fascist group, Mehmet Ali Ağca. He recovered and continued his papacy for a number of years. On April 2, 2005, he spoke his final words and died.

Following his death, a number of clergy and laymen began calling him John Paul the Great, the fourth pope to receive that accolade. The process to make him a saint almost immediately after his death. In 2009, he was made "Venerable," and officially became a saint in 2014.

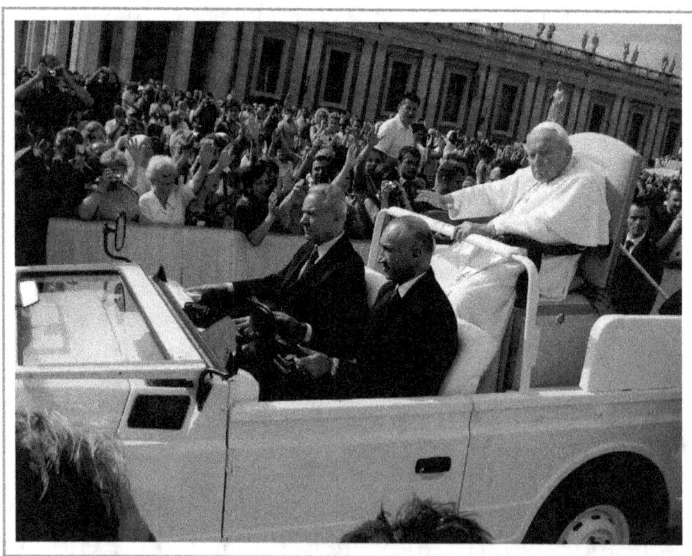

Pope John Paul II in 2004 (Photo:Thalion77, CC BY-SA 2.5)

More May 18 Birthdays

Architecture

Walter Gropius, German architect who founded the "Bauhaus school" and a pioneer of modernist architecture. *(1883)*

The Bauhaus-Archiv in Berlin, designed by Walter Gropius (Photo:Thalion77, CC BY-SA 2.5)

Art and Photography

Don Martin *(illustration right),* cartoonist for *MAD* magazine. *(1931)*

Bill Everett, comic book writer who created such characters as the Sub-Mariner and Daredevil; member of the Will Eisner Hall of Fame. *(1917)*

Gertrude Käsebier, influential photographer known for her portraits of Native Americans of motherhood as well as the promotion of photography as a career for women. *(1852)*

Portrait of Martine McCulloch by Gertrude Käsebier (1910)

Mathew Brady, pioneering photographer best known for his Civil War photographs. *(1822)*

Self portrait sof Mathew Brady in 1875

Crime and Punishment

Giovanni Falcone, Italian judge and prosecutor known for his campaign against the Sicilian Mafia, who later assassinated him. *(1939)*

Exploration and Adventure

Jessica Watson, Australian sailor who received the Order of Australia for completing a southern hemisphere solo circumnavigation at the age of 16. *(1993)*

Jeana Yeager, co pilot of the Rutan Voyager on its record-setting first non-stop, non-refueled flight around the world. (She is not related to aviator Chuck Yeager.) *(1952)*

Government

Walter Sisulu, South African anti-apartheid activist and leader in the African National Congress; jailed for 25 years for political activity. *(1912)*

Jacob Javits, New York City politician who served in both houses of Congress; namesake of New York's Javits Convention Center. *(1904)*

Nicholas II (Николай II), last Tsar of Russia, forced to abdicate after the February Revolution, killed along with his family by orders of the new Bolshevik government. *(1868 *)*

The last Russian Imperial family. From left to right: Olga, Maria, **Nicholas II,** Alexandra Fyodorovna, Anastasia, Alexei, and Tatiana,

---

* His birthdate is also given as "O.S. May 6." At the time of his birth, Russia used the Julian "Old Style" calendar, but converted to the modern Gregorian calendar shortly before the death of Nicholas II. As a result, his original birthday of May 6 is the same as May 18 on the Gregorian calendar. For more on different calendar types, see "What Day of the Week is May 18?"

Letters

Francis Bellamy, Christian socialist minister and author best known for writing the original US Pledge of Allegience. *(1855)*

Omar Khayyám (عمر خیام), Persian mathematician, astronomer, philosopher, and poet, best known for his *Rubaiyat*, which contains the famous stanza, "A Book of Verses underneath the Bough / A Jug of Wine, a Loaf of Bread—and Thou / Beside me singing in the Wilderness / And oh, Wilderness is Paradise enow." *(1048)*

Music and Dance

Martika, singer-songwriter known for her 1989 hit "Toy Soldiers." *(1969)*

Mark Mothersbaugh, singer-songwriter and composer best known as the lead singer of the new wave band Devo, as well as for his many themes for television series and movies, including *Rugrat*s and *The Lego Movie. (1950)*

Joe Bonsall, gospel and country singer for the Oak Ridge Boys. *(1948)*

Albert Hammond, singer-songwriter and producer who wrote such hits as "Nothing's Gonna Stop Us Now" and "To All the Girls I've Loved Before" as well as "It Never Rains in Southern California" which he also performed. *(1944)*

Mark Mothersbaugh as lead singer of Devo
(Credit: LivePict.com, CC BY-SA 3.0)

Margot Fonteyn, prima ballerina for the Royal Ballet; appeared in several television specials. *(1919)*

Perry Como, singer and television personality who hosted several television musical variety shows and numerous Christmas specials; received the Grammy Lifetime Achievement Award for his work. *(1912)* *(Photo next page.)*

Ezio Pinza, Italian opera singer who later crossed over into Broadway musical theater; appeared in several films and hosted a daytime television musical program. *(1892)*

Perry Como

Tina Fey (Credit: Mingle Media TV)

Performing Arts

Tina Fey, comedian, actress, and writer best known for the sitcom *30 Rock* and for her work on *Saturday Night Live*. *(1970)*

Miriam Margolyes, English character actress best known as Professor Sprout in the *Harry Potter* film series. *(1941)*

Dwayne Hickman, actor best known as the title character in the sitcom *The Many Loves of Dobie Gillis*. *(1934)*

The cast of *The Many Loves of Dobie Gillis* (1960). Left to right: **Dwayne Hickman**, Danielle De Metz, and Bob Denver

Robert Morse, star of the Broadway hit and film version of *How to Succeed in Business Without Really Trying,* and as Bertram Cooper on the television series *Mad Men. (1931)*

Pernell Roberts, actor best known as Adam Cartwright on the television series *Bonanza* and as the title character in *Trapper John, M. D.. (1928)*

The cast of *Bonanza* (1962). From top: Lorne Greene, Dan Blocker, Michael Landon, and **Pernell Roberts**

Bill Macy, actor best known as the husband of the title character on the 1970s sitcom *Maude. (1922)*

Richard Brooks, filmmaker and novelist who directed such films as *Blackboard Jungle, Cat on a Hot Tin Roof, Elmer Gantry, In Cold Blood,* and *Looking for Mr. Goodbar. (1912)*

Meredith Wilson, composer and playwright best known for his Broadway musical (and later film) *The Music Man. (1902) (See also page 46.)*

Frank Capra, filmmaker known for such classics as *It Happened One Night, You Can't Take It With You, Mr. Smith Goes to Washington,* and the Christmas perennial *It's a Wonderful Life. (1897) (Photo page 12)*

Science

Vincent du Vigneaud, American biochemist who received the 1955 Nobel Prize in Chemistry for his work on oxytocin. *(1901)*

Bertrand Russell, important philosopher, mathematician, and social critic who received the Nobel Prize in Literature. His groundbreaking *Principia Mathematica,* which established a logical basis for mathematics, is famous for a several hundred page long proof that 1+1=2. *(1872[†])*

[†] "The above proposition," he wrote, "is occasionally useful."

Oliver Heaviside, self-taught physicist and mathematician who made major contributions to the study of electrical circuits. The Heaviside layer of ionized gas in the atmosphere, which he predicted to exist, is named for him. *(1850)*

Sports and Games

Jens Bergensten, video game designer best known for creating the game *Minecraft. (1979)*

Jari Kurri, five-time Stanley Cup champion inducted into the Hockey Hall of Fame; named one of the "100 Greatest NHL Players in History." *(1960)*

Brent Ashton, most traded player in the history of the National Hockey League during his fourteen season career. *(1960)*

Reggie Jackson, right fielder for 21 seasons in Major League Baseball; member of the Baseball Hall of Fame. *(1946)*

Brooks Robinson, third baseman with the Baltimore Orioles for 23 seasons; member of the Baseball Hall of Fame. *(1937)*

Fred Perry, former World No. 1 tennis player who was the first to win a "Career Grand Slam" of all four singles titles. *(1909)*

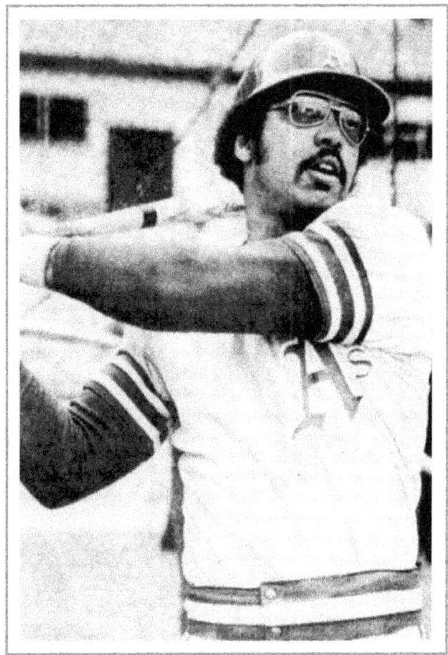

Reggie Jackson (1973)

Brooks Robinson (1955)

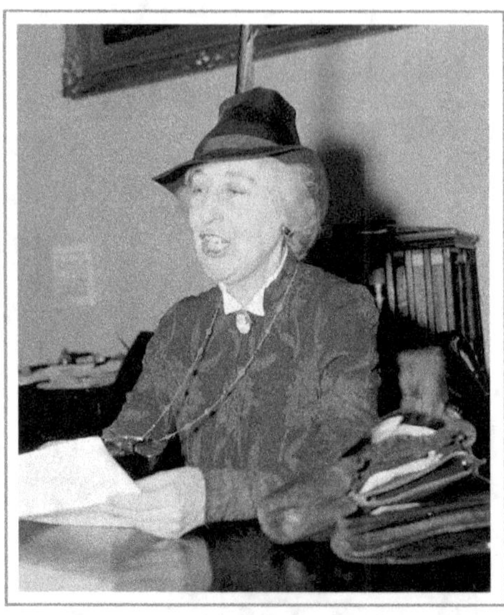

Jeannette Rankin (Credit: Harris & Ewing)

Mary McLeod Bethune (Credit: Carl Van Vechten)

Who Died on May 18?

Business and Media

Roger Ailes, founder and Chairman/CEO of Fox News, as well as a media consultant for several Republican presidential campaigns. *(2017)*

Elijah Craig, entrepreneur in the area that later became the state of Kentucky, sometimes credited as the inventor of bourbon whiskey. *(1808)*

Civil Rights and Women's Rights

Jeannette Rankin, first woman to hold national office in the United States as a member of Congress for the state of Montana; helped initiate the legislation that became the 19th Amendment (votes for women); lifelong pacifist who was the only member to vote against declaring war on Japan after Pearl Harbor. *(1973)*

Mary McLeod Bethune, African-American educator and activist, advisor on civil rights to FDR known as the "First Lady of the Struggle" for her activities. *(1955)*

Exploration and Adventure

Wubbo Ockels, Dutch physicist and astronaut who flew on the *Challenger* STS-61-A shuttle mission and became the first Dutch citizen in space. *(2014)*

Jacques Marquette, Jesuit missionary and explorer who founded the first European settlement in Michigan, and was one of the first to explore and map the northern portion of the Mississippi River. *(1675)*

Government and Military

Túpac Amaru II, led an Andean uprising against the Spanish in Peru, considered an inspiration and key figure in the Peruvian struggle for independence and indigenous rights. *(1781)*

Letters

William Saroyan, novelist and playwright best known for *The Human Comedy;* won a Pulitzer Prize and an Oscar for his writing. *(1981)*

Music

Chris Cornell, musician and singer-songwriter best known as lead vocalist for Soundgarden and Audioslave; wrote and performed the theme for the 2006 James Bond film *Casino Royale.* *(2017)*

Túpac Amaru II

Elvin Jones, jazz drummer in the post-bop era, working with such artists as John Coltrane; member of the *Modern Drummer* Hall of Fame. *(2004)*

Gustav Mahler, German late Romantic composer and conductor known for his controversial modernist pieces. *(1911)*

Performing Arts

Elisha Cook Jr., actor best remembered as Wilmer the gunsel in the 1941 Humphrey Bogart film *The Maltese Falcon. (1995)*

Elisha Cook, Jr., in *Dark Mountain* (1944)

Jill Ireland, actress best known for her fifteen films with husband Charles Bronson. *(1990)*

Arthur O'Connell, nominated twice for the Academy Award for Best Supporting Actor for the films *Picnic* and *Anatomy of a Murder. (1981)*

Science

Pierre-Gilles de Gennes, French scientist who won the 1991 Nobel Prize in Physics. *(2007)*

Charles Louis Alphonse Laveran, won the 1907 Nobel Prize in Physiology or Medicine for discovering the parasitic causes of infectious diseases such as malaria. *(1922)*

Sports

Ernie Davis, first African-American winner of the Heisman Trophy and member of the College Football Hall of Fame; the 2008 film *The Express* is based on his life. *(1963)*

Hal Chase, first baseman and manager for several MLB teams, called by Babe Ruth "the best first baseman ever." Alleged to have gambled on baseball games and thrown games in which he played, and was eventually banned from the game. *(1947)*

Quote of the Day

"If a composer could say what he had to say in words he would not bother trying to say it in music."

Gustav Mahler, composer
died May 18, 1911

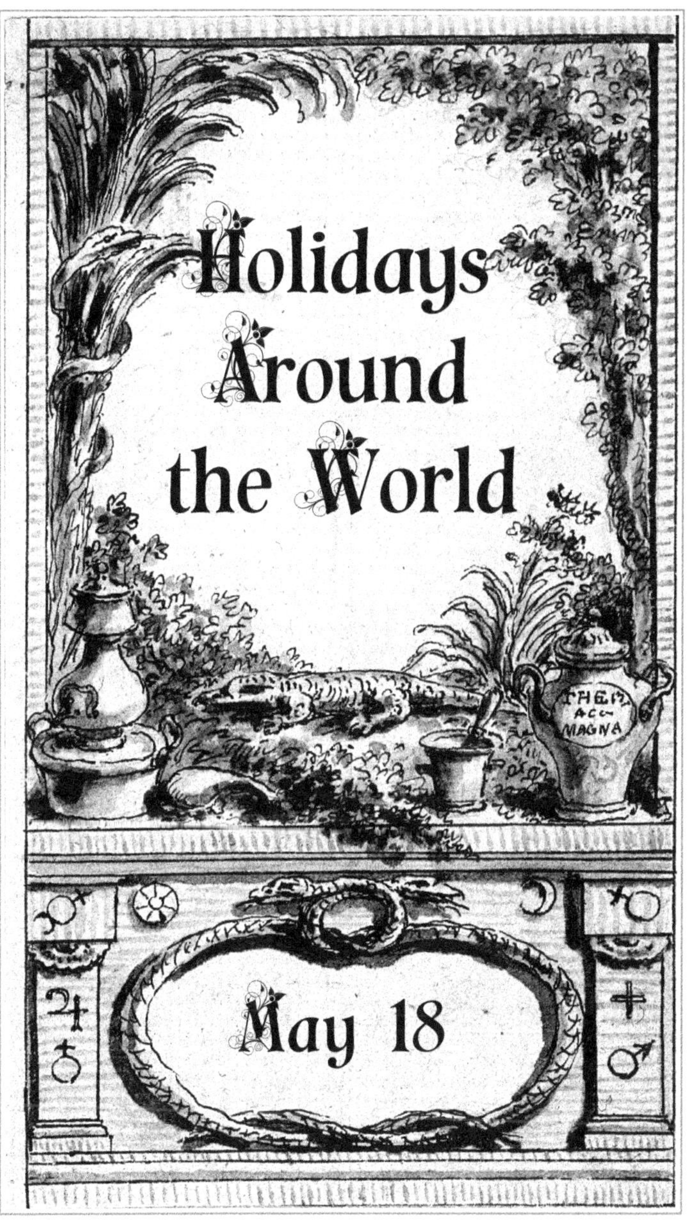

Holidays
Around
the World

May 18

The Battle of Las Piedras, by Diógenes Hecquet

May 18 Holidays and Celebrations

If you're looking for a reason to take your special day off, you should know that every single day is a holiday somewhere in the world! Here's some of what you can celebrate on May 18!

General Events

Battle of Las Piedras Day (Uruguay)

A key battle in the revolution for Uruguayan independence, the Battle of Las Piedras, took place May 18, 1811, ending in a total victory for the revolutionary forces. It is a public holiday in Uruguay. *(See also page 6.)*

Day of Remembrance of Crimean Tatar Genocide (Ukraine)

On May 18, 1944, an ethnic cleansing of Tatars from Crimea took place by order of Soviet leader Joseph Stalin, with nearly 200,000 deported to what is today Uzbekistan. Tens of thousands died during the deportation and in exile. Their fate is honored in the Ukraine each May 18.

Day of Revival, Unity, and the Poetry of Magtymguly (Turkmenistan)

Turkmeinistan honors the poet, spiritual leader, and advocate for Turkmen independence, Magtymugulu Pyragy, on the anniversary of his birth, May 18, 1724.

Independence Day (Somaliland)
Somaliland celebrates its declaration of independence from Somalia on May 18, 1991.

International Museum Day (worldwide)
The International Council of Museums promotes awareness of the role museums play in the development of society.

Jour du Drapeau et de l'Université (Haiti)
The nation of Haiti celebrates its educational system and the 1803 creation of its flag on Flag and Universities' Day, held May 18.

The flag of Haiti

Mullivaikkal Remembrance Day
(முள்ளிவாய்க்கால் நினைவு நாள்) (Tamil)
The Sri Lankan Tamil people commemorate those who died in their civil war on May 18, the anniversary of the end of the war in 2009. It is named for the site of the last battle of the war.

Remembrance Day (ජාතික රණවිරු සැමරුම් උළෙල) (Sri Lanka)

The nation of Sri Lanka commemorates its war heroes and others who died in the Sri Lankan Civil War. It was previously known as Victory Day.

World AIDS Vaccine Day (international)

World AIDS Vaccine Day raises awareness of the urgent need for a vaccine to prevent HIV and AIDS.

Religious Feast Days and Holidays

Saint Days

Each day in the year is considered a feast day for one or more saints. They are somewhat different in western Christianity (Catholicism and many forms of Protestantism) and in eastern (Orthodox) Christianity. There are many others; this is a selection.

In *Western Christianity*, May 18 is the feast day of Saints Ælfgifu of Shaftesbury, Eric IX of Sweden, Felix of Cantalice, Pope John I, and Venantius of Camerino.

In *Eastern Orthodox Christianity*, it is also the commemoration of Saints Anastaso of Leukadion, Martinian of Areovinthus, Feredarius, Macarius Glukharev of the Altai, and John Gashkevich. (These saints are honored on May 5 by "Old Calendrists.‡")

---

‡ "Old Calendrists" use the older Julian calendar rather than the modern Gregorian calendar for liturgical purposes. April 13 on the Julian calendar is the same day as March 31 on the Gregorian calendar. For more about the different types of calendars, see "What Day of the Week is May 18?"

Food Holidays

In the United States, almost every day of the year is dedicated to a particular food — some days honor more than one!. Sponsored by manufacturers, retailers, farmers, or simply fans, these days are often proclaimed by the President, Congress, state governors, or mayors.

In the US, May 18 is **National Cheese Souffle Day.** A soufflé.is made with egg yolks and beaten egg whites that puffs up when cooked. A variety of flavors are added, including cheese, herbs, vegetables, or for sweet soufflés, fruits, chocolate, and jam.

A cheese soufflé (Photo: Breville, CC BY-SA 2.0)

When May 18 falls on the third Friday of the month, it's also **National Pizza Party Day**. If it's the third Saturday, it's **World Whisky Day.**

Honorary Food Months: *In addition, the entire month of May is used to celebrate numerous foods. Here's a list of food-related observances in the month of May!*

- National Beef Month
- National Barbecue Month
- National Loaded Potato Month
- National Chocolate Custard Month
- Month National Egg Month
- National Hamburger Month
- National Salad Month
- National Salsa Month
- National Strawberry Month
- National Raisin Week (first week in May)
- National Herb Week (first week in May)

Strawberries, by Deborah Griscom Passmore

Honorary Months

Presidents, Congresses, and nations around the world issue proclamations recognizing particular months to honor certain causes. These events generally fall in May, though honorary months do come and go.

Three places to get up to date information are Wikipedia, the current edition of Chase's Calendar of Events *or the website Brownielocks. Here are some honorary designations for May.*

- Asian Pacific American Heritage Month
- Better Hearing and Speech Month
- Celiac Awareness Month
- Community Action Awareness Month (North Dakota)
- Cystic Fibrosis Awareness Month
- Ehlers-Danlos Syndrome Awareness Month
- Flores de Mayo (Philippines)
- Garden for Wildlife Month
- Haitian Heritage Month
- Hepatitis Awareness Month
- International Mediterranean Diet Month
- Jewish American Heritage Month
- Kaamatan harvest festival
- Mental Health Awareness Month
- Month of the Blessed Virgin Mary. (Catholicism)
- National ALS Awareness Month
- National Brain Tumor Awareness Month
- National Corps Member Appreciation Month
- National Electrical Safety Month (United States)

- National Foster Care Month (United States)
- National Golf Month
- National Innovators Month
- National Military Appreciation Month
- National Mobility Awareness Month (United States, Canada)
- National Moving Month
- National Osteoporosis Month
- National Pet Month (United Kingdom)
- National Smile Month (United Kingdom)
- National Stroke Awareness Month
- National Water Safety Month
- New Zealand Music Month (New Zealand)
- Older Americans Month
- Season of Emancipation (April 14 to August 23) (Barbados)
- Skin Cancer Awareness Month
- South Asian Heritage Month (International)
- World Trade Month

Moveable and Multi-Day Events

Some events take place over a specific week or time period. Start and finish dates may vary from year to year. Some events occur on different days each year (such as "fourth Saturday of a month"). These events sometimes take place on or include May 18.

Last Monday Before May 25
- National Patriots' Day (Quebec)
- Victoria Day (Canada)

Monday On or Before May 24
- Victoria Day (Scotland)

Third Monday
- Discovery Day (Cayman Islands)

Third Friday
- Arbor Day (Prince Edward Island)
- National Defense Transportation Day
- Endangered Species Day
- O. Henry Pun-Off Day
- NASCAR Day

Third Saturday
- The Preakness Stakes, second jewel in the Triple Crown of horse racing, takes place
- Culture Freedom Day
- Armed Forces Day (US)

Third Sunday
- Commemoration Day of Fallen Soldiers
- Father's Day (Tonga)

Just for Fun

Anybody can make up a holiday, and many people do! While none of these are officially recognized and some may come and go, here are a few more holidays for May 18.

- Buy a Musical Instrument Day (in honor of Meredith Wilson, composer and playwright who created *The Music Man,* born May 18, 1902) *(See page 27.)*
- I Love Reese's Day
- Mother Whistler Day
- Visit Your Relatives Day

An Arrangement in Grey and Black (Whistler's Mother), by James McNeill Whistler

Quote of the Day

"Rough winds do shake the
darling buds of May."

William Shakespeare, Sonnet XVIII

About
the
Month
of
May
THEP.
ACL.
MAGNA

"May," from the *Brevarium Grimani* by Simon Bening (c.1510)

May: The Fifth Month

"Then came fair May, the fairest maid on ground,
Deck'd all with dainties of the season's pride,
And throwing flowers out of her lap around. ."

— Edward Spenser, *The Faerie Queene, Book VII*

According to many scholars, the month of May takes its name from the Roman goddess Maia, an earth goddess who was the mother of Mercury. The poet Ovid, on the other hand, claimed that May took its name from the Latin maiores, meaning ancestors. In either case, the month of May in ancient Rome was marked by sacrifices to Maia, and her son Mercury was honored on the Ides of May (May 15).

May is the fifth month of the year in both Julian and Gregorian calendars. It was originally the third month in ancient Rome, because the new year began on March 1. Although Julius Caesar changed the length of several months during his great calendar reform (the Julian calendar), the length of May has remained constant at 31 days.

In the northern hemisphere, May occurs in the springtime, and in the southern hemisphere, May takes place in fall. Strangely, no other month begins or ends on the same day of the week as the beginning or ending of May, although January of the following year always begins and ends on the same day of the week as this year's May.

May in Other Cultures

The month of April has different names in different languages. Some nations use calendars other than the Gregorian, and their months may overlap with April. Still, they often have a word for April itself.

- In Latin and Old English, the month of May was named *Maius*, and it is *Mai* in French.

- In Arabic, the month is مايو, pronounced *māyū*.

- In Chinese, the equivalent month is 五月.

- Croatians call the month *svibanj* and in Czech it is *květen*. In Finland, it is *toukokuu*.

- The Jewish month of *Sivan* (סִיוָן) normally falls in May-June.

- It is the third month of the Jewish ecclesiastical year.

- The Irish called the month *bealtaine*, and it marked the beginning of summer.

- Slovenians call May *veliki traven*, or the month of the big grass.

May Sayings and Superstitions

Here are some sayings and superstitions associated with the month of May.

Never buy a broom in May.

"Wash a blanket in May / Wash a dear one away."

Cats born in May will bring snakes into the house.

"Those who bathe in May / Will soon be laid in clay."

Marriage in May

May is an unlucky month for getting married.

> "Marry in May and rue the day, but marry in April if you can, joy for maiden and for man."

> Which day? "Monday for wealth, Tuesday for health, Wednesday the best day of all, Thursday for losses, Friday for crosses, Saturday for no luck at all."

May Symbols

Birthstone: Emerald

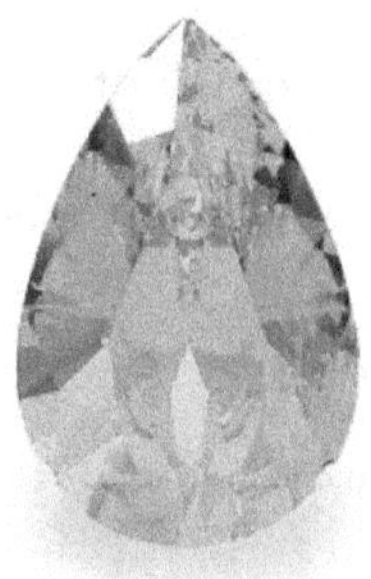

Birth Flowers: Lily of the Valley and Hawthorn

Lily of the Valley

Common Hawthorn

"May," by Eugène Grasset

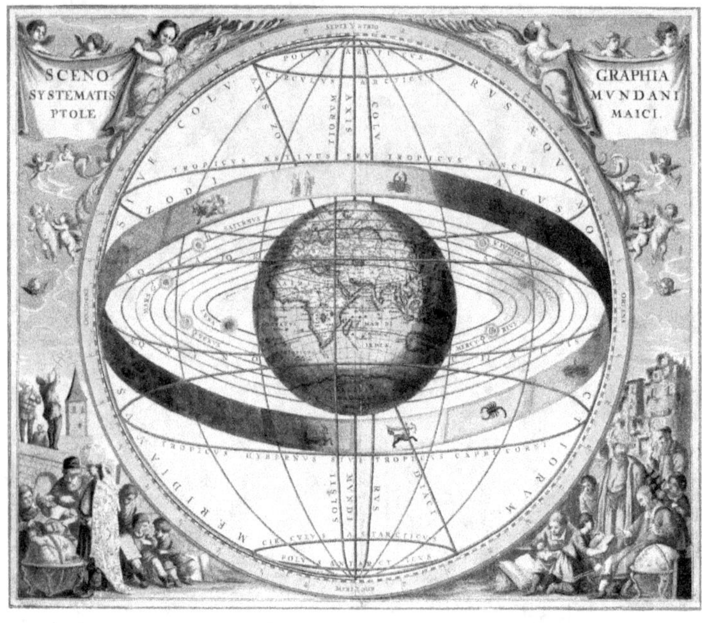

Scenography of the Ptolemaic Cosmography, by Johannes van Loon, based on Andreas Cellarius's *Harmonia Macrocosmica,* 1660

May 18 Zodiac Signs

From the perspective of someone on Earth, the Sun appears to move through the sky throughout the year, along a path astronomers call the *ecliptic plane.* The ecliptic plane is divided into twelve constellations, known as the zodiac, based on traditionally observed patterns of stars. On your birthday, you can't see your constellation, because it's in the daytime sky.

The zodiac was first developed by Babylonian astronomers about 2,500 years ago. Because they were unaware that the Earth wobbles like a spinning top (known as *precession*), they didn't make allowance for the fact that the Sun's path through the zodiac changes over time.

That means there are now two sets of dates for your birth sign. The *tropical dates* are the original Babylonian dates; the *sidereal dates* tell you where the Sun actually appears as it moves along its annual path.

May 18, however, is one of the few days in the year in which the tropical and sidereal signs are the same: **Taurus.**

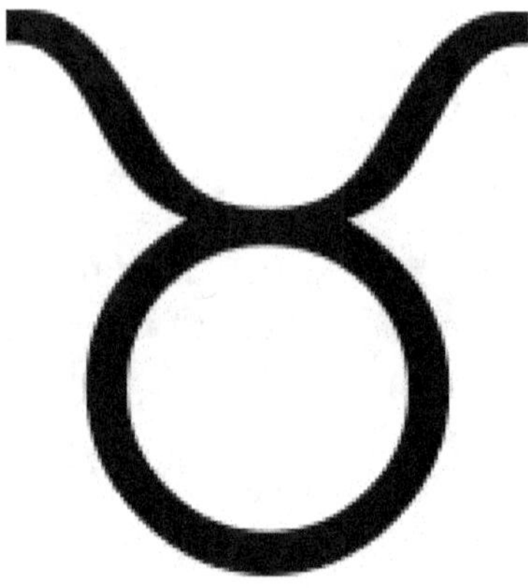

Taurus

Tropical April 21 to May 21
Sidereal May 16 to June 15

The astrological sign of Taurus (the Bull) originated in ancient Mesopotamia, who called it the "Bull of Heaven," and believed it to be a symbol of strong will, perseverance, and determination. The Egyptians knew it as Hathor (the Cow Goddess), who was the goddess of beauty, love, and happiness. That's why Roman astrologers said that Taurus was ruled by Venus, their goddess of beauty.

In astrology, Taurus is an Earth sign, compatible with Cancer, Capricorn, and Pisces. Taureans are supposed to be headstrong, powerful, and hard-working.

The Sign of Taurus, by Giovanni Maria Falconetto (Courtesy Palazzo d'Arco)

Illustration by Edward Penfield

What Day of the Week is May 18?

On what day of the week does May 18 fall?

Surprisingly, this isn't an easy question. Because the calendar year is 365 days long (366 in leap years), it doesn't divide evenly by the seven days of the week.

Also, the Earth goes around the Sun in about 365-1/4 days, so a calendar tends to drift over time. That's why the same date falls on different weekdays in different years.

This is made even more complicated by a change in calendars that took place in 1582. Our modern calendar has its roots in ancient Rome, in a calendar reform conducted by Julius Caesar. Caesar commissioned mathematicians to attack the problem, and they came up with the idea of leap years, and thus standardized the calendar for centuries to come. This was called the Julian calendar.

Over time, however, the small errors in Caesar's calculation compounded. That's why Pope Gregory XIII commissioned the Gregorian calendar, used in most of the world today. Some countries converted in 1582, when the calendar was first developed; some converted later; other still haven't changed.

Gregorian and Julian aren't the only types of calendars. The Hebrew year, the Islamic year, and many other calendars are used in different parts of the world and among different people.

You can convert Gregorian dates to other calendars, including the Hebrew calendar, the Islamic calendar, and even the Mayan calendar by visiting the Fourmilab Calendar Converter at http:// www.fourmilab.ch/documents/calendar/.

Chinese calendar systems are quite complex and have changed several times; a full discussion is far beyond the scope of this book. If you're interested, you can find information here: http:// www.hermetic.ch/cal_stud/chinese_cal.htm.

On Names and Dates

Historians use "CE" (Common Era) and "BCE" (Before the Common Era) instead of the more common "AD" (Anno Domini, or Year of Our Lord) and "BC" (Before Christ), reflecting the fact that the year-numbering system established by the Gregorian calendar is used throughout the world in many countries not culturally Christian.

The CE/BCE designation dates back to at least 1708, and has been adopted as a standard by the United Nations and the Universal Postal Union. Because this series of books covers events and people of all nations and cultures, we use the CE/BCE terms.

The abbreviation "O.S." ("Old Style") and "N.S." ("New Style") on some dates refers to the fact that the Russian Empire (in particular) did not switch from the Julian to the Gregorian calendar at the same time as the rest of Europe, and therefore some figures and events have two dates.

Also, in the Julian calendar in England in the 16th century, the year began on March 25 rather than January 1. To avoid confusion with Gregorian dates, dates between January and March were often written using both years.

People and events whose original names are not in the Western alphabet have their native names (where possible) in the appropriate script shown in parenthesis. If you are using an e-reader to access an electronic version of this book, all characters don't always display on all devices.

A 50-year brass perpetual calendar.

Quote of the Day

"Time is an illusion, lunchtime doubly so."

Douglas Adams,
from *The Hitchhiker's Guide to the Galaxy*

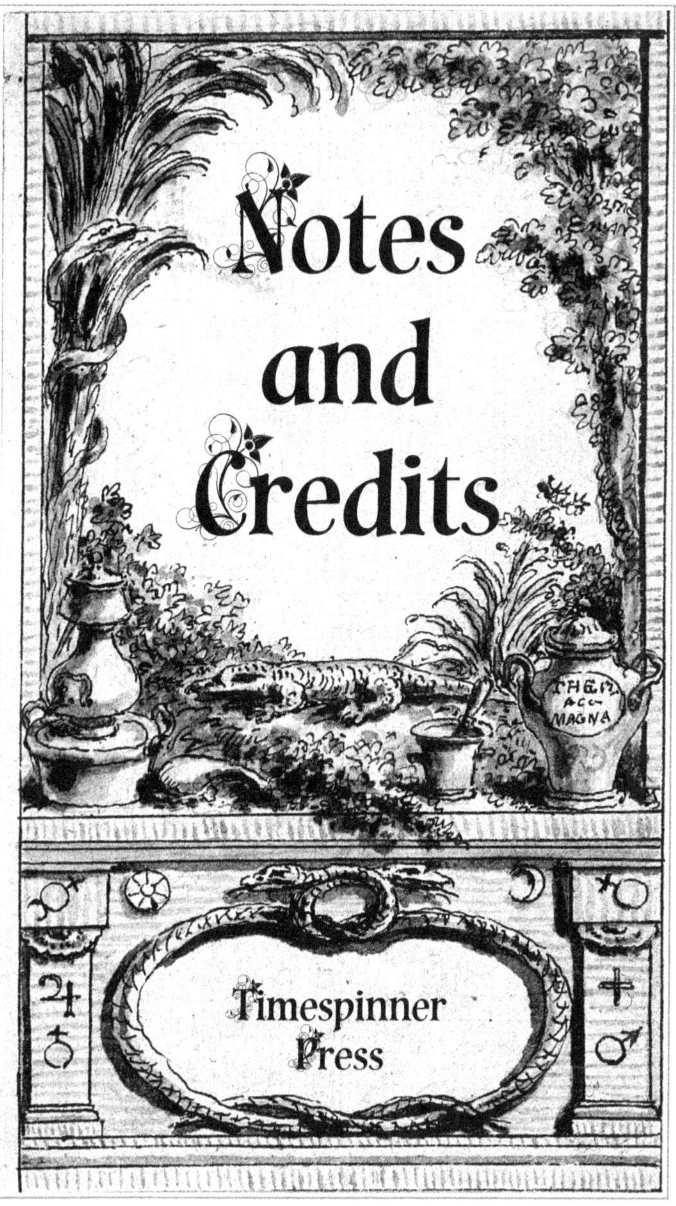

Notes
and
Credits

THES
ACC
MAGNA

Timespinner
Press

Cartoon by John T. McCutcheon

Copyright, Credit, and Contact

Follow Us

Our blog "This Day in History" (http://timespinnerpress.com/this-day-in-history/) features short articles on events and people associated with each day, and updates several times each week. Also subscribe to the "Quote of the Day" at http://timespinnerpress.com/quote-of-the-day/. You can get daily links by following us on Facebook at TimespinnerPress, or on Twitter as @sidewisethinker.

Contact Us

Find an error or a format problem? Want information about the series, about us, or about when the volume for your special day might be available? Please email us at editor@timespinnerpress.com. (We also take requests if your special day isn't yet complete. Please give us at least six weeks' notice if possible.)

Sources

We owe a great debt to Wikipedia, which is our first stop for research. We attempt to make independent confirmation of all important dates and facts through a variety of other sources.

Other sources we frequently use include the Library of Congress; "on this day" listings from *Encyclopedia Britannica*, the *New York Times*, and the BBC; Omniglot for the names of months in other languages; *Chase's Calendar of Events*; and, of course, the always essential Google.

All art and photographs are either in the public domain, used under a Creative Commons license, or with a "fair use" justification, and most frequently come from Wikimedia Commons and the Library of Congress Prints and Photographs Division.

Attribution is provided where possible, or as requested by the copyright owner, or when there is particular historical significance, listed below. For information about any particular illustration or photograph, please contact us.

Credits

1. The 1812 painting *The Emperor Napoleon in His Study at the Tuileries* by Jacques-Louis David is in the public domain because its copyright has expired. The original is in the collection of the National Gallery of Art, Washington, DC; the image is courtesy Google Art Project.

2. The illustration of the month of May used on the back cover is from the French Gothic illuminated manuscript *Les Très Riches Heures du duc de Berry* by the Limbourg Brothers, Jean Colombe, and an intermediate painter whose name is lost to history. It is in the public domain because its copyright has expired.

3. The box graphic used on the first page is from a 1916 pamphlet entitled "Divorce versus Democracy" authored by G. K. Chesterton, originally published in London by the Society of St. Peter and St. Paul. It is in the public domain in the US because it was published prior to 1923, and is in the public domain in all countries (including the country of origin) in which the copyright time is the author's life plus 70 years or less.

4. The graphic design for the section pages in this book is from a design originally created for a pharmacy label. It is courtesy of Wellcome Images (ICV No 11073, photo V0010813), and is used here under CC BY-SA 4.0.

5. The painting *The Coronation of Emperor Napoleon I and Coronation of the Empress Josephine in the Notre-Dame de Paris, December 2, 1804,* by Jacques-Louis Davi and Georges Rouget

was created between 1805 and 1807 and is in the public domain because its copyright has expired. The original is in collection of the Louvre Museum, Paris. It has been cropped.

6. The photograph of Napoleon's Tomb is by Remy Overkempe and is used here under CC BY-SA 3.0.

7. The painting *The Siege of Acre* by Dominique Papety was created circa 1840 and is in the public domain because its copyright has expired.

8. The 1860 photograph of Abraham Lincoln by Alexander Hessler is in the public domain because its copyright has expired.

9. The 1926 photograph of Aimee Semple McPherson in the hospital was taken for International News Photos (now United Press International). It is in the public domain because it was published in the United States between 1923 and 1963, and although there may or may not have been a copyright notice, the copyright was not renewed.

10. The 1953 photograph of Jackie Cochran and Chuck Yeager is in the public domain as a work created by an employee of the US government as part of that person's official duties.

11. The painting "May" by Hans Thoma is from his book *Festkalender*. It is in the public domain because it was published prior to 1923 and its copyright has expired.

12. The 2011 photograph of Pope John Paul II was taken by Rafic Abou Fadel and is used here under CC BY-SA 3.0. It has been cropped.

13. The 2004 photograph of Pope John Paul II was taken by Thalion77, and is used here under CC BY-SA 2.5.

14. The 2011 photograph of the Bauhaus-Archiv was taken by Eisenacher, and is used here under CC BY-SA 3.0.

15. The illustration by Don Martin is presumably copyrighted. It is used here under "fair use" provisions of the copyright code. It illustrates a person of historical significance in a way to make clear who he is, no free equivalent is available, and the image is of a size and resolution unsuitable for the creation of counterfeit goods.

16. The 1910 portrait of Martine McCulloch by Gertrude Käsebier is in the collection of the Denver Art Museum

(1984.696). It is in the public domain because its copyright has expired.

17. The 1875 self-portrait of Mathew Brady is in the public domain because its copyright has expired. It is from the Brady-Handy Collection at the Library of Congress, LC-DIG-cwpbh-03798. It has been cropped.

18. The 1913 photograph of the family of Nicholas II of Russia was created by the Levitsky Studio in Livadiya, and is in the collection of the Hermitage Museum in St. Petersburg, Russia. It is in the public domain in Russia, its country of origin, because it was published prior to November 7, 1913, and in the US because it was published prior to January 1, 1923.

19. The 2008 photograph of Devo is from LivePict.com, and is used here under CC BY-SA 3.0.

20. The 1956 publicity photograph of Perry Como is in the public domain because it was first published in the United States between 1923 and 1977 without a copyright notice. Traditionally, publicity photographs are not copyrighted because of the way in which they are intended to be used.

21. The 2014 photograph of Tina Fey at the premiere of *Muppets Most Wanted* is by Mingle Media TV, and is used here under CC BY-SA 2.0. It has been cropped.

22. The 1960 publicity photograph from *The Many Loves of Dobie Gillis* is in the public domain because it was first published in the United States between 1923 and 1977 without a copyright notice.

23. The 1973 photograph of Reggie Jackson is by United Press International. It is in the public domain because it was published in the United States between 1923 and 1963, and although there may or may not have been a copyright notice, the copyright was not renewed.

24. The 1962 publicity photograph from *Bonanza* is in the public domain because it was first published in the United States between 1923 and 1977 without a copyright notice.

25. The 1956 official rookie photograph of Brooks Robinson is in the public domain because it was first published in the

United States between 1923 and 1977 without a copyright notice.

26. The 1939 photograph of Jeannette Rankin is from the Harris & Ewing collection at the Library of Congress (digital ID hec.26014). According to the Library, there are no known copyright restrictions on this work. It has been cropped.

27. The 1949 photograph of Mary McLeod Bethune is by Carl Van Vechten, and is part of the Carl Van Vechten photograph collection at the Library of Congress (digital ID van. 5a51728). According to the Library, there are no known copyright restrictions on this work.

28. The 19th century portrait of Tupac Amaru II is in the public domain because its copyright has expired.

29. The 1944 photograph of Elisha Cook, Jr., in the film *Dark Mountain* is in the public domain because it was published in the United States between 1923 and 1963, and although there may or may not have been a copyright notice, the copyright was not renewed.

30. The 1896 illustration of the Battle of Las Piedras by Diógenes Hecquet is in the public domain because its copyright has expired. The illustration has been cropped.

31. The Haitian flag is not an object of copyright.

32. The 2013 photograph of a cheese soufflé is by Breville, and is used here under CC BY-SA 2.0

33. The 1890 painting of strawberries by Deborah Griscom Passmore is in the public domain as a work created by an employee of the US government as part of that person's official duties.

34. The painting *An Arrangement in Grey and Black* by James Whistler is in the public domain because its copyright has expired. The painting is in the collection of the Musée d'Orsay, Paris.

35. The painting "May" by Simon Bening is from the *Brevarium Grimani*, circa 1510, and is in the public domain because its copyright has expired.

36. The 1815 woodcut of a proposal is in the public domain because its copyright has expired.

37. The photograph of an emerald was taken by Les Facettes and is used here under the CC BY-SA 3.0 license.

38. The photograph of a lily of the valley (*convallaria majalis*) is by H. Zell and is used here under the CC BY-SA 3.0 license.

39. The photograph of a hawthorn (*Crataegus monogyna*) is by Sannse and is used here under the CC BY-SA 3.0 license.

40. The 1896 drawing "May" by Eugène Grasset is in the public domain because its copyright has expired.

41. The celestial sphere is from *Scenography of the Ptolemaic Cosmography*, by Johannes van Loon, based on Andreas Cellarius's *Harmonia Macrocosmica*, 1660. It is in the public domain because its copyright has expired.

42. The fresco *The Sign of Taurus* by Giovanni Maria Falconetto was created between 1510 and 1520, and is in the public domain because its copyright has expired. It can be seen in the Palazzo d'Arco, Mantua, Italy.

43. The 1906 automobile calendar is by Edward Penfield, and is in the collection of the Library of Congress Prints and Photographs Division. It is in the public domain because its copyright has expired.

44. The 50-year perpetual calendar photograph is in the public domain.

45. The cartoon by John T. McCutcheon is from his 1905 collection *The Mysterious Stranger and Other Cartoons by John T. McCutcheon*. It is in the public domain because its copyright has expired.

46. The painting of May by Simon Bening was created circa 1483 and is in the public domain because its copyright has expired.

47. The 1945 US Army poster promoting mosquito repellent by artist Frank Mack is in the public domain as a work created by an employee of the US government as part of that person's official duties.

License Description and Terms

Aside from material purely in the public domain, photographs and other material in this book are used under specific licenses permitting free use, usually with an attribution requirement. For full text and terms of these licenses, click or enter the appropriate links below. If you believe there is an error in the copyright status or attribution of any of these images, please email us.

- Creative Commons Attribution 2.0 Generic (CC-BY 2.0): http://creativecommons.org/licenses/by/2.0/deed.en
- Creative Commons Attribution-Share Alike 3.0 Generic (CC-BY-SA 3.0): http://creativecommons.org/licenses/by-sa/3.0/
- Creative Commons Attribution-Share Alike 2.5 Generic (CC-BY-SA 2.5): http://creativecommons.org/licenses/by-sa/2.5/deed.en
- Creative Commons Attribution-Share Alike 2.0 Generic (CC-BY-SA 2.0): http://creativecommons.org/licenses/by/2.0/deed.en
- Creative Commons Attribution-Share Alike 1.0 Generic (CC-BY-SA 1.0): http://creativecommons.org/licenses/by-sa/1.0/deed.en
- CC0 1.0 Universal (CC0 1.0) Public Domain Dedication (CC0 1.0) http://creativecommons.org/publicdomain/zero/1.0/deed.en
- GNU Free Documentation License (GFDL): http://en.wikipedia.org/wiki/Wikipedia:Text_of_the_GNU_Free_Documentation_License
- License Art Libre (Free Art License): http://artlibre.org

May, by Simon Bening

Other Books from Timespinner Press

The Story of a Special Day

Michael Dobson

A series of (eventually) 366 volumes covering everything that happened on your special day! Events, births, deaths, quotes, holidays, and much more. It's like a birthday card they'll never throw away!

US$7.95 print / US$2.99 ebook.

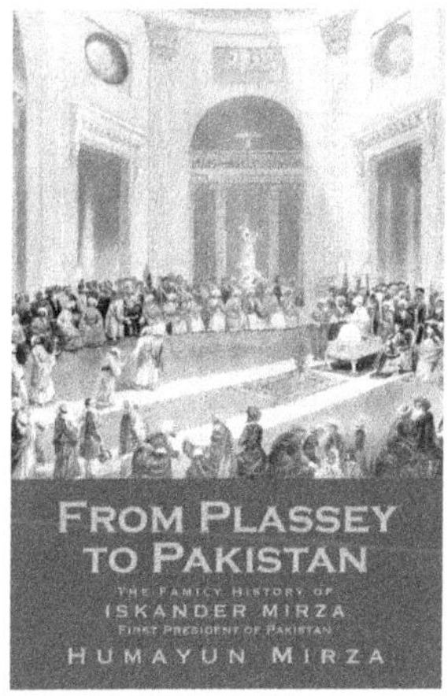

From Plassey to Pakistan

Humayun Mirza

The history of British Colonial India and the formation of Pakistan from the unique perspective of the son of Pakistan's first president and last of the royal line of Bengal, Bihar, and Orissa! This unique historical document tells the inside story of this distinguished family, including the detailed story of the coup that toppled his father from power!

US$27.95 print

A Whole New Navy: America's War in the Pacific

Miles Durr

The most comprehensive and detailed description of America's naval war in the Pacific ever—every battle, every ship, every task force and every task group from Pearl Harbor through the Japanese surrender! A must-have for the collection of every World War II buff!

US$29.95 print

Improbable History: The Weird, the Obscure, and the Strangely Important

edited by Michael Dobson

From the birth of Western civilization to the rescue of Apollo 13, from the Leaning Tower of Pisa to Florence's Duomo, history has often turned on small, improbable details. Whatever happened to the ancient Samaritan people? Why did a fortuitous rainstorm allow the British to conquer India? How did an air raid in Italy lead to the development of chemotherapy? What happened when Albert Einstein met Adolf Hitler on the streets of Berlin? How did the Japanese manage to attack the US mainland using balloons? A cast of award-winning writers tackle some of the strangest tales in history!

US$19.95 print

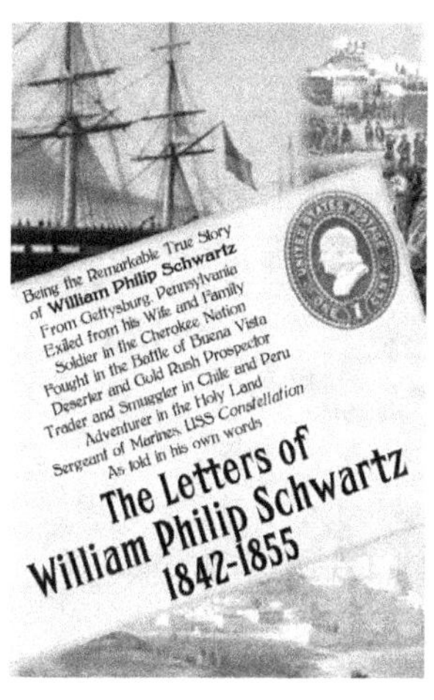

The Letters of William Philip Schwartz 1842-1855

edited by John F. Schwartz

The 19th century soldier and adventurer William Philip Schwartz wrote a series of vivid and detailed letters chronicling his adventures in the Indian Wars, the Mexican-American War, the Gold Rush, and his term as Marine sergeant aboard the USS Constellation. A pioneer in photography, he took *the first known war photographs*. An unforgettable first-hand look into life in the 19th century!

US$17.95 print

Timespinner
Press

www.timespinnerpress.com

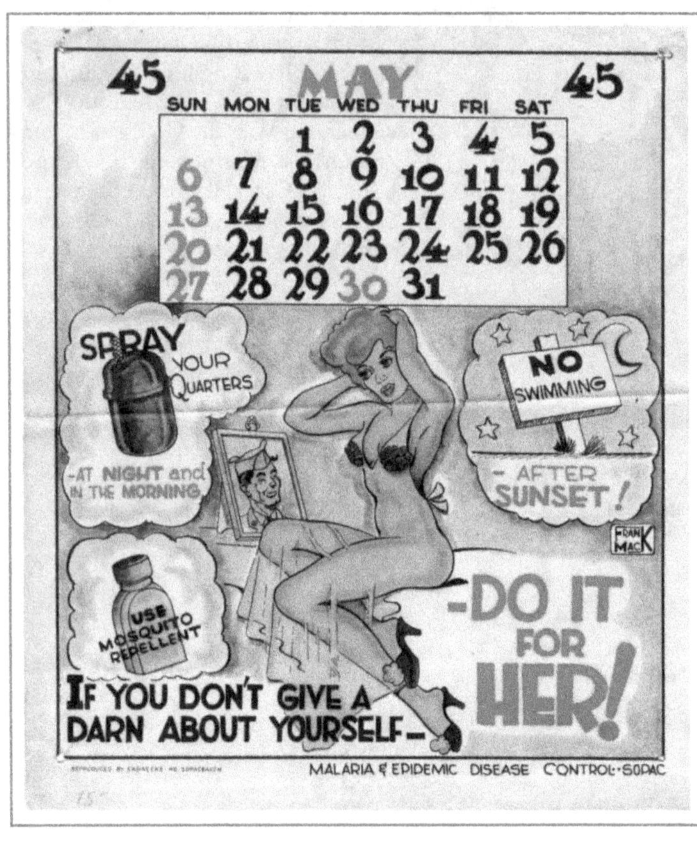

A 1945 US Army poster for the month of May promoting use of
mosquito repellent to control malaria and other diseases, by artist
Frank Mack. (Courtesy National Library of Medicine)